BARING SOLES in FASHION

A BEHIND THE SEAMS LOOK AT BEAUTY & FASHION
Tyron Barrington

Characters by Tyron Barrington

with illustrations by Kephera Ife

Baring Soles in Fashion
A Behind the Seams Look at Beauty & Fashion
Tyron Barrington

Published by Barrington Publishing Group
Miami Beach, Florida

Characters by Tyron Barrington
with illustrations by Kephera Ife

Creative Director: Marina Barlage

ISBN: 978-0-9995650-1-8 (paperback)

ATTENTION CORPORATIONS, UNIVERSITIES, COLLEGES AND PROFESSIONAL ORGANIZATIONS: Quantity discounts are available on bulk purchases of this book for educational, gift purposes, or as premiums for increasing magazine subscriptions or renewals. Special books or book excerpts can also be created to fit specific needs. For information, please contact Barrington Publishing Group, Tyron@Barringtonmgt.com.

BARING SOLES IN FASHION

For Jace, Lolo & Jaya

and for the Dreamers in all of us

THE **DREAM** ISSUE:

Editor-In-Chief

THE SUPERMODELS:

Fear as herself

Doubt as herself

Worry as herself

Bound aka Superbound as herself

Faith as herself

SUMMARY AND DEFINITIONS:

DREAM:

Represents our desires and goals in life

THE RACE:

Represents the steps we take in life to accomplish our goals for Dream

SEPTEMBER:

The deadline we set to achieve our Dream

ONCE UPON

A TIME...

in the glamorous world of fashion stood the world's most famous supermodels, ready to run the most important race of the year, the race for the cover of Dream, the desire of every model!

And this cover is for September, the most prestigious of them all. Each year, the cover has become the prize that every model, celebrity and personality aspires to. It's the one that propels them from obscurity to elite superstar status and the envy of the fashion world. It's the one the darlings of fashion anxiously await in the mail or at the newsstand kiosk, anticipating the big reveal: who will receive the honor and distinction THIS year?

FEAR and DOUBT — chief Dream blockers

Their Story: Sisters Fear and Doubt are the world's reigning supermodels and have been for centuries! They have visions of Dream, but their dreams are to block and prevent anyone from achieving or attaining their own Dream. They are the epitome of beauty and reinvention.

They come into fashion and wear each other's masks in each season's collection more than any other supermodels to come their way. They have had many covers and disguises over the years, but they have to keep recreating their image season after season! Many in the industry know that they are dangerous, but they still wind up beguiled by their charm and fashion sense. Once again they are back in the starting block…

WORRY—another Dream blocker

As her name implies, Worry is a major supermodel on the fashion scene.

Worry always has issues about her life, home, what she's eating, what people are saying about her, if she's thin enough…she never stops worrying! She has so much anxiety about whether or not she is perfect that she doesn't enjoy being a model. She takes her place at the starting line…

BOUND — a model in bondage to old designer collections

Bound's name and title says it all! She is one of the oldest of the Supermodels.

Although constantly troubled by Fear and Doubt, who are her best friends, she knows that in order to stay on top and keep her 'covers', she has to keep reinventing herself. Her bondage to past designer collections, however has had her hitting many hurdles in life, from addiction and anxiety to depression. She is afraid to "step out" of these old collections to achieve anything more than her past Dream covers.

They cling to her as everything else does! Her subtle beauty is dangerous and deceiving.

FAITH

Unlike Fear and Doubt, Worry and Bound, Faith has always been in the race but without much fanfare. You see, Faith has always run a different kind of race throughout life. She is always in Dream and is known as "the Upsetter" because she's totally unpredictable! You never know when or where she will pop up. This is because she is sent from God, the Editor-in Chief of Life! Faith is quite confident that she can live up to her name and win the cover of Dream. She has watched Fear and Doubt "go at it" for quite a while and has decided that since both of them will be eyeing each other, she will stay in her lane and run a great race!

She is going to enjoy it, no matter what comes her way!

As usual, some of the world's most famous supermodels will be on the starting block ready to run the race of their life to achieve their cover of this year's Dream magazine.

The model's journeys for Dream have caused hurt and bitterness along the way, especially among fellow models, agents, photographers and the style teams that consistently hide their flaws and imperfections through the magic of makeup.

Their beautiful yet deceptive looks allow them to steal many pages and covers of Dream…except for the elusive September issue.

In the middle of the race is the relative unknown supermodel called Faith. She pops up unexpectedly in life's daily walk by surprising everyone when they least expect her to!

NOW...

…as this story goes, you may see something in each of these models that reminds you of someone you know—maybe yourself.

To understand this race and how it all came about, you have to go back to the Editor-in-Chief of Dream, the Creator of Life.

Each day, the Editor, who has fashioned lives from each of their births, sends out directives to everyone with visions of Dream inviting them to the starting block to run their race to achieving their dreams. But, the Editor also knows that in order for anyone to see their dreams come to fruition, they have to get past Fear & Doubt by letting go of their bondage to Bound, and the anxieties of life brought on by Worry.

The Editor knows that many are called to the race, but few ever make it to the finish. For that reason, he hopes that this year each person who enters the race for Dream will get past all the supermodels who are in their way. He hopes that when they hit hurdles, they will get up and continue to run the race of their lives; that their eyes will stay focused on their dreams; that they will stay in their own lanes and not look back, but instead look ahead to the finish line: their goal of Dream!

FEAR & DOUBT
ASPIRE TO BE
ON THE COVER
OF DREAM, THE
SEPTEMBER
ISSUE.

THE FALL COLLECTION

It's the collection the Editor hopes the models will not be tempted to wear during this race. It might be beautiful to look at, but there's a price to pay for that beauty. The Fall Collection clothes its models in designer Envy, Bitterness, Anxiety and Resentment – things that can easily tear and break them down.

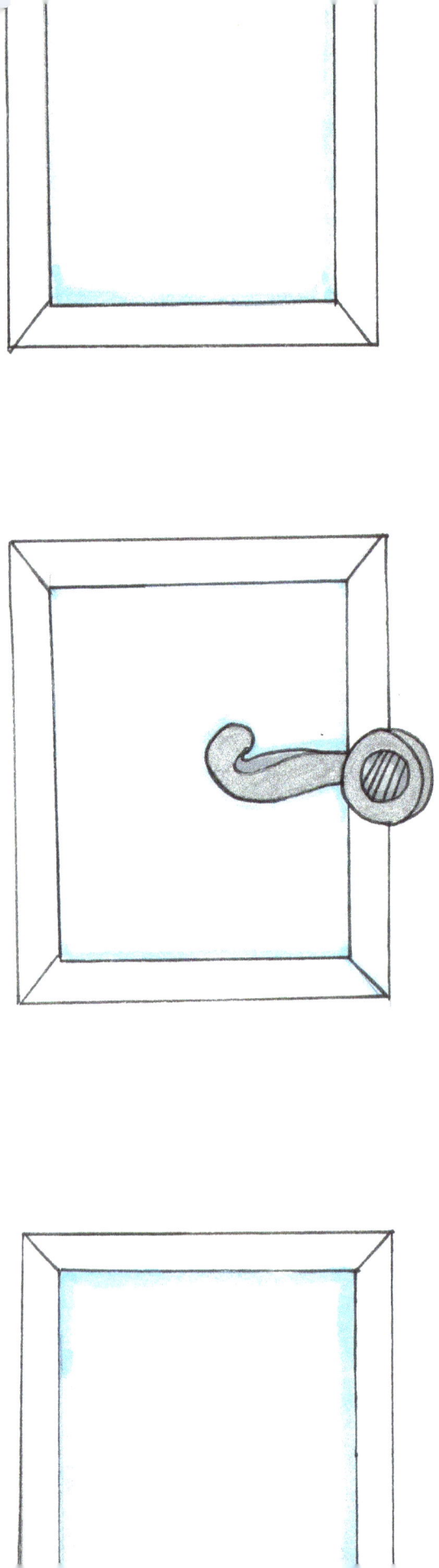

SOMETIMES, CHANGING EVERYTHING

JUST MAKES YOU
FORGET WHO
YOU ARE . . .

…but this is the price Fear and Doubt are willing to pay. They have moved their beloved Fall Collection into new designer bags, containing new shoes and accessories like the bracelet of addiction, rings of loneliness, hats of rage, gloves of bitterness, corset of aging, an array of eyeglasses of envy and strife, and the scarf of hurt and rejection. These are the tricks that have made them so chic on all of their previous covers…but which have also made them so insecure and full of pain.

ON
YOUR

MARK

The race is about to begin. They're all on their marks and in their lanes getting ready to run the race for Dream! Each model's heart and mind are on the issues of their past and what may come of their future. Bound is thinking about all her baggage. Worry is filled with anxiety: Will she trip? Break a heel? Meanwhile, Faith's heart is bowed, praying for wisdom, knowledge and strength to run an amazing race and win the cover of Dream.

THEY'RE ON
THEIR STARTING
BLOCKS!

Faith is surprised to see both Fear and Doubt carrying so many
bags and wearing so many layers of outfits. She knows it's hard
to run a successful race in a Fall Collection.

Meanwhile, everyone else is dazzled — even Worry is excited to
see their new collection and fascinating new hairdos!

THE JET SET GETS

...SET TO RUN!

FALSE START!

Fear has jumped the gun, trying to get a head start on the competition and intimidate the other supermodels! But unbeknownst to many, her false starts in life are due to her own insecurities, along with that continued fear of life and what others may think of her.

Jumping
the Gun

Once the Editor gives us our vision of Dream, there is always a period of preparation, training and waiting. No one who desires the cover of Dream gets it immediately; it takes patience, determination and hard work to achieve goals!

Finally, they're off!

The time has come for the Supermodels to take the necessary

steps to make their dreams come true.

Unsurprisingly, both Fear and Doubt have taken an early lead,

which is their usual tactic in life in order to stay ahead and

intimidate the other models.

Wearing their designer heels, frontrunners Fear and Doubt use their charm to block the others. They are notorious for this! Fear always uses the past of other models as a way to remind them of their flaws and hidden secrets, while Doubt uses fear of the future to prevent them from going forward. These are their greatest weapons in blocking others from achieving their Dream cover while trying to win another cover for themselves.

Meanwhile, Bound and Worry have already fallen behind…

BUT, THEN... DISASTER!

HITTING LIFE'S

HURDLES:

Busy looking back to make sure the other models are intimidated, Doubt missteps and falls over one of life's hurdles! Her tendency to look behind and not at the future has caused disaster! "Ouch!" winces Fear with a grin and an insincere look on her face; secretly, laughing at her sister's pain.

Fear can relate to the hurdles of life though; the many distractions of her past have caused her to take plenty of falls herself! But in order for her or Doubt to ever make it to the finish line, they both have to learn to let go of their past failures and look ahead.

Meanwhile, as Doubt crashes facedown, there's a gasp. Everyone realizes that Doubt, who had the lead in the race, is fallen and bruised.

Her once immaculately made-up face now revealed the true troubles of her past… and who she really is. She begins to cry, streaking her mascara.

YOU CAN'T STAY DOWN FOR LONG…

The Editor knows that it is okay to cry when you hit some of life's hurdles…but instead of staying down and feeling sorry for yourself, it is best to get back up, sort out the hemlines, change the make-up artist, if need be, and put on a brave new face and continue to run the race to the finish! The cover of Dream is yet to come! It is important to grieve failures, but not to let the grief consume or destroy your will to achieve your goals.

DOUBT'S ACHILLES HEELS

Doubt's heels came from the hottest designers, but now they are her "Achilles heels": weaknesses that she can't overcome. Their beauty is now cracked and broken. She has worn so many designer pairs due to her need to hide her flaws that it's taken a toll on her body.

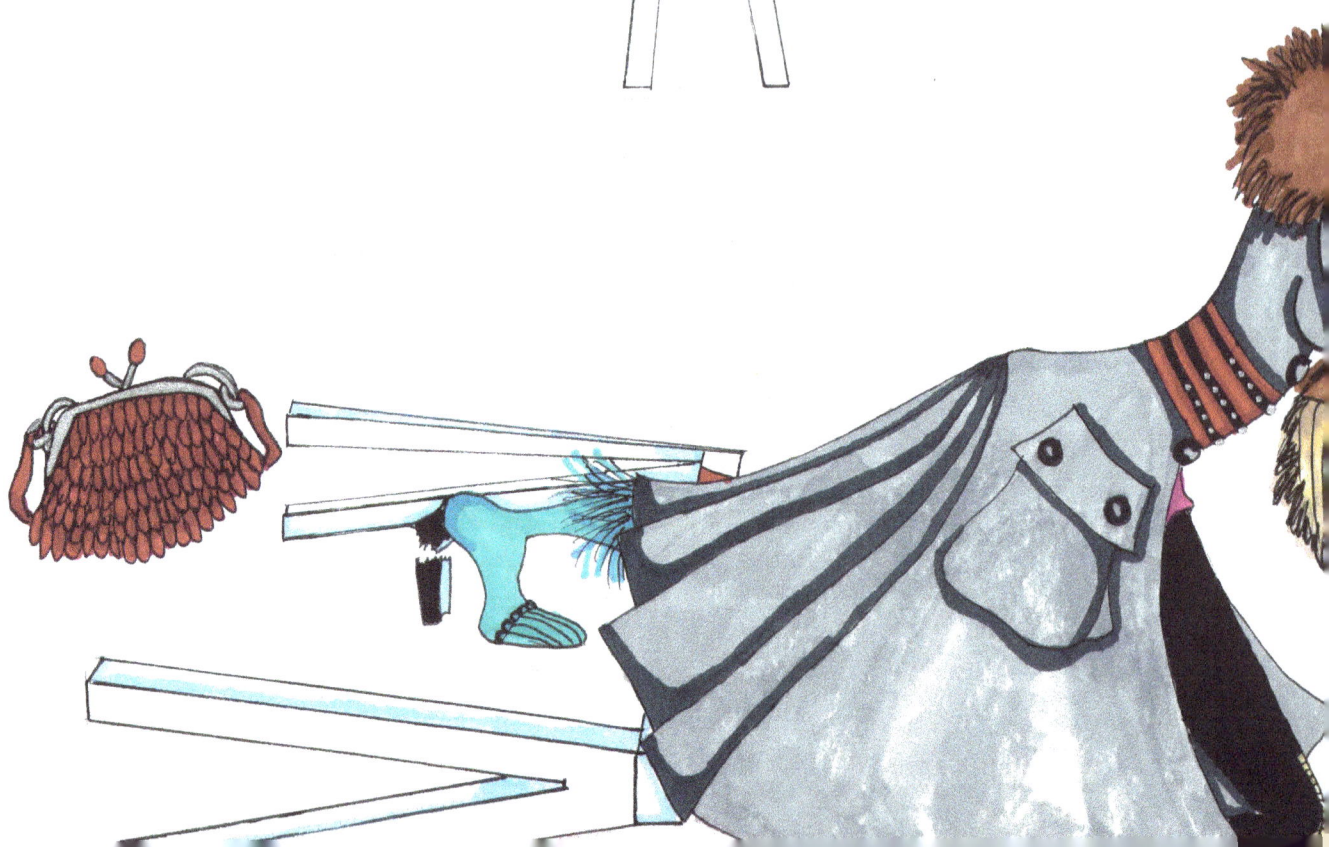

DOUBT IS DOWN…

Fear, seeing what has happened, has kept her stride and moved on, determined to stay ahead of Faith, who has been nipping at her heels throughout the race. Faith was wise enough to show up without any baggage or fanfare, dressed in a light spring collection, knowing that she could not run a strong race while weighed down by anything pricey, ornate or heavy. She has learned to trust the Editor's judgment and has come prepared to win!

GET UP... & CONTINUE RUNNING!

Writhing in pain, with broken heels, seeing the rest of the supermodels passing her, Doubt leaps to her feet and runs. She realizes that to get to the finish line, she must let go of all the makeup, designer collections and baggage she's been carrying around. But can she catch up to the leaders?

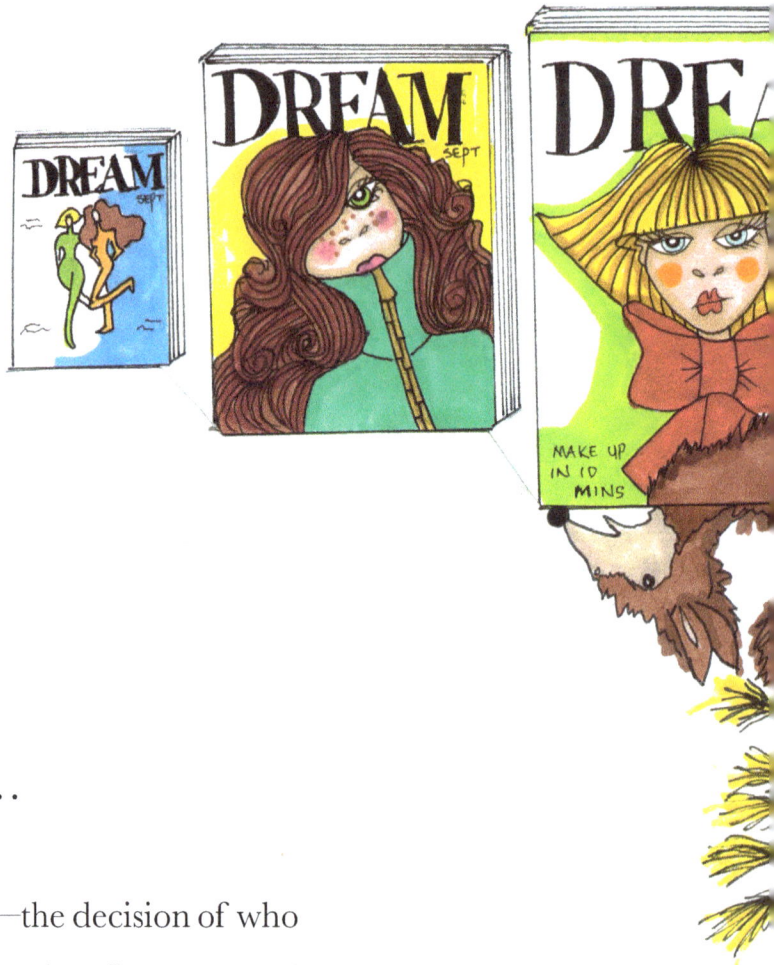

INTO THE FINAL TURN…

Now the models can see the finish line—the decision of who will make the exclusive cover of September Dream—and as they do, the models remember their past covers. Back then, they were not known as Fear and Doubt. But as they got older, their attitudes changed. Their dreams became disheartening as the top designers, photographers, stylists and editors stopped calling them for work as much as they once had.

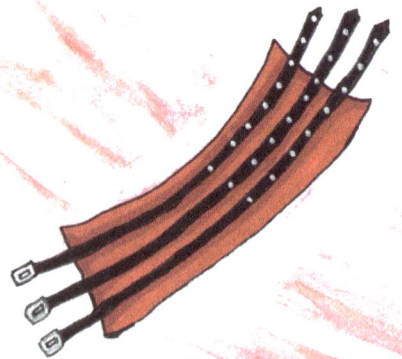

LETTING GO OF THE PAST &

SPRINTING TO THE END!

BOOTS
COME OFF!
ACCESSORIES
GO FLYING!
THE
ONLOOKERS
ROAR!

The Editor knows that for any of these models to achieve this cover of Dream, they have to shake off the old Fall Collection and cut the hemlines that are distracting and keeping them down so that they can move forward towards achieving their dreams.

Change is hard, but there's no reaching the finish without it! The models know that it's a new season for obtaining the cover of Dream—if only they can let go of the heels of their past that weigh them down. They've seen Faith moving easily and fast, and now they're ready to do the same!

THE
HOME
STRE

As they close the distance to the finish, the models work to prevent anyone else from getting ahead of them. They can taste their victory, but they know they have to defeat Faith in order to win the cover of September Dream.

Coming into the final stretch of the race, they are barely one hemline ahead of Faith, with Worry coming up fast from the rear!

Sensing Faith gaining more strength with each stride, they decide to step up their own effort. Stride for stride and heel for heel, they're getting closer, with hemlines flying—the battle is heating up! With only one hurdle before the finish line, the crowd is on its feet, looking to see who will be first!

TCH

A GASP…

The onlookers realize that Worry has fallen behind
and is out of the race! Anxious that she does not have
what it takes to win, she has lost momentum. Her
worries have caught up with her once again as her
mind drifts off course.

She is alone and behind everyone now, even Bound.

Up ahead, Fear and Doubt can see the finish line!

So can Faith—but only one can win…

CROSSING THE

FINISH LINE

Fear, Doubt and Faith are neck-and-neck to the wire! They're making a final dash to the finish line! With flashbulbs going off all around, the speedy supermodels break the tape…

E PHOTO FINISH

E PHOTO FINISH

E PHOTO FINISH

E PHOTO FINISH

E PHOTO FINISH

E PHOTO FINISH

E PHOTO FINISH

E PHOTO FINISH

E PHOTO FINISH

THE PHOTO FINI
THE PHOTO FINI
THE PHOTO FINI
THE PHOTO FINI
THE PHOTO FINI
THE PHOTO FINI
THE PHOTO FINI
THE PHOTO FINI
THE PHOTO FINI

THE WINNER IS…FAITH!

The photo finish revealed that Faith was consistent in believing that she could make the cover of Dream and had done what the Editor had hoped by bringing a fresh new look and feel of hope and happiness. Because of this, she nipped the other models at the finish line!

As the Editor tells us, in order to achieve one's Dream, it takes faith and belief in oneself, not Bound and Worry, and certainly not Fear and Doubt!

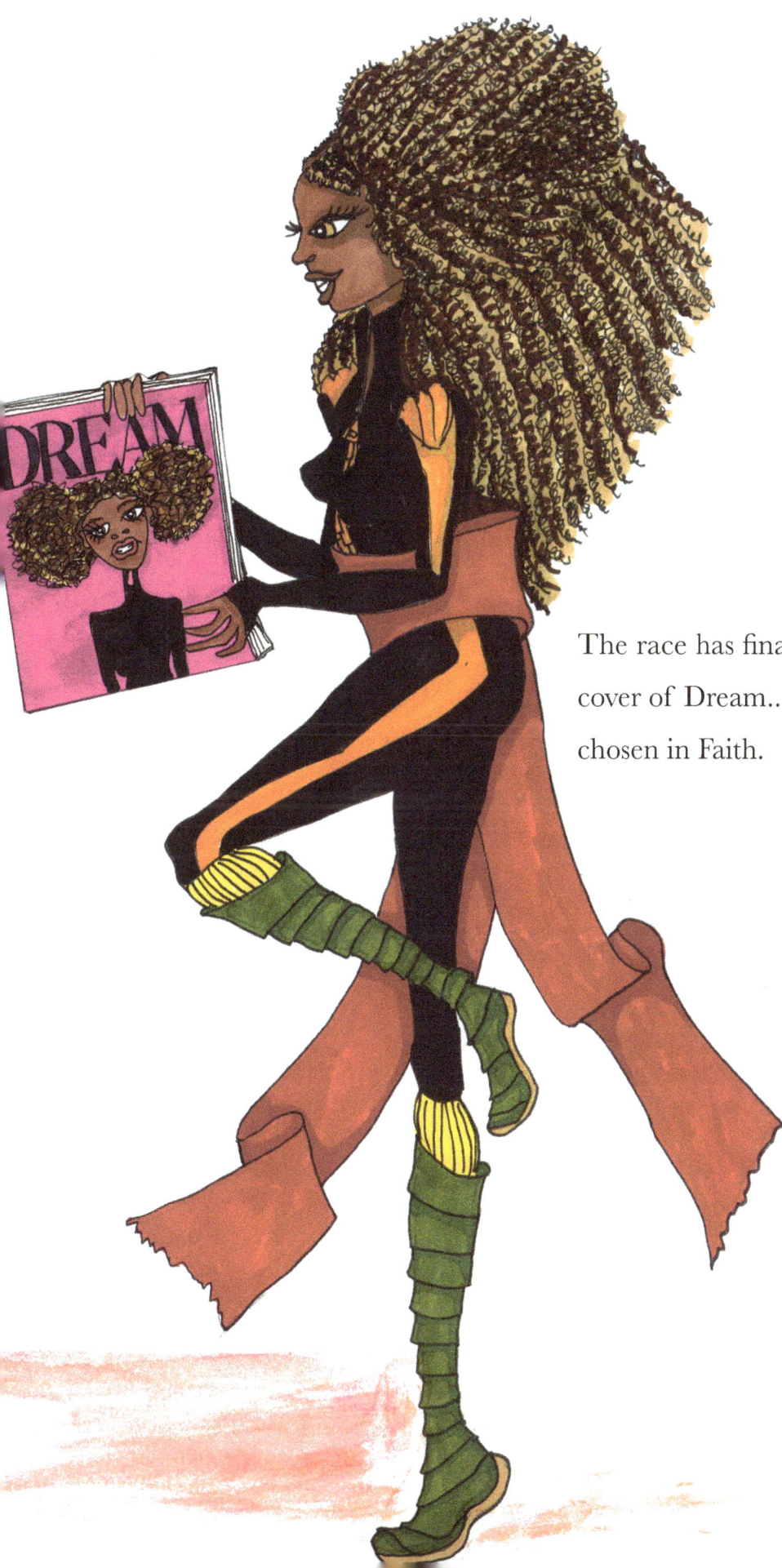

The race has finally ended for September's cover of Dream... and a winner has been chosen in Faith.

THE
REW

ARD

RECEIVING DREAM

The race is not for the swift, but for those who endure to the end; who keeps their eyes and heart focused on their Dream by staying in their own lane and looking to the most important Editor in Chief of Life, for guidance.

The fashion world is filled with messages that encourage us to only see our flaws, hold onto baggage from the past and believe that we can only succeed by undermining others. This book was created to show that those messages do not lead to success or happiness. Faith, hope, compassion and love, however, will lead us to whatever God has planned for us, whether that is the cover of Dream that appears far away. Run your race with faith, pride and obedience to God, the Editor-in-Chief of life, and you'll always win!

THANK YOU.

First to my Lord, Jesus Christ, for giving me DREAM.

To Jaya for the few years you shared with us on earth, you were a gift from God. Though physically unable to walk properly, you always tried to run, yet each time you kept falling, but always tried again. May all your falls be an example for those with 'battered soles, and broken heels', to know that they can rise again.

Je t'aime our beautiful Fifi. RIP.

Thank you to Kephera for being my eyes in bringing these beautiful characters to life, to my incredible editor Tim Vandehey for making the story flow, to Marina Barlage my creative director who made the pages beautiful, Peter Bertino for constant and valuable help in proof reading the book, to my incredible agent Kirsten Neuhaus, Wendy Goya for always checking and double checking everything, and to all my brothers and sisters, nieces and nephews, aunts and uncles all over the world, friends and neighbors, The Brooklyn Tabernacle Church, Pastor Maria at Unbroken Chain Church, Rev. Garth at Miami Beach Community Church - gone but not forgotten, thank you.

I love and adore each of you.

God Bless.
TYRON BARRINGTON

Mife
MINISTRY IN FASHION
+EDUCATION

Founded in 2012 as a nonprofit 501 (c) (3) organization, Ministry in Fashion Education's ("MIFE") mission is to promote education to support youth entering the fashion, arts & entertainment industry, through mentoring, connecting and internships. Education takes place in a variety of formats including talks with current leading experts in the field of modeling, beauty, and television. Topics are focused on protecting youth from exploitation, cultural exchange, women as leaders, faith, and minority inclusion.

To learn more about these initiatives and the foundation, visit www.mifetalks.com

TYRON BARRINGTON is a fashion industry expert.

A former Top Model Agent and now Fashion Producer and Casting Director, for clients such as AVON, REVLON, LEVI'S, TARGET, L'OREAL, LAURA MERCIER, to name a few. He's worked with celebrities such as KYLIE JENNER, VANESSA HUDGENS, LUCY HALE, ASHLEY GREENE, LAUREN CONRAD, KAT GRAHAM, JAMIE CHUNG, ROCSI DIAZ, TYSON BECKFORD, MATTHEW FOX, CARRE OTIS, EMMA HEMING-WILLIS, etc.

He is also the author of "THE LORD IS MY AGENT…AND, HE ONLY TAKES 10%".

He's also the President of MiFE & MiFE TALKS events, a non-profit organization that mentors teens, and young adults entering the fashion & entertainment industry, as well as bringing awareness to issues such as FGM (Female Genital Mutilation), Mental Health and Fashion, etc.

He's been featured on ABC NIGHTLINE, as well as in the NY POST, and the DAILY NEWS, as well as on numerous television series including I CAN MAKE YOU A SUPERMODEL in Holland, and the United Kingdom.

For more information, contact: Tyron@Barringtonmgt.com

TYRON BARRINGTON

BARRINGTON GROUP…
MIAMI BEACH – NEW YORK, HAVANA & THE CARIBBEAN
INSTAGRAM: @tybarrington
EMAIL: tyron@barringtonmgt.com
WEB: http://www.barringtonmgt.com

www.ingramcontent.com/pod-product-compliance
Lightning Source LLC
Chambersburg PA
CBHW042351030426
42336CB00026B/3446